To:_____

From:_____

God, grant me . . .

> Courage and hope
>   for every day,
> Faith to guide me
>   along my way,
> Understanding
>   and wisdom too,
> And grace to accept
>   what life gives me to do.

THE HELEN STEINER RICE FOUNDATION

When someone does a kindness
it always seems to me
That's the way God up in heaven
would like us all to be . . .

Whatever the celebration, whatever the day, whatever the event, whatever the occasion, Helen Steiner Rice possessed the ability to express the appropriate feeling for that particular moment. A happening became happier, a sentiment more sentimental, a memory more memorable because of her deep sensitivity and ability to put into understandable language the emotion being experienced. Her positive attitude, her concern for others, and her love of God are identifiable threads woven into her life, her work . . . and even her death.

Prior to Mrs. Rice's passing, she established the HELEN STEINER RICE FOUNDATION, a nonprofit corporation that awards grants to worthy charitable programs assisting the elderly and the needy.

Royalties from the sale of this book will add to the financial capabilities of the HELEN STEINER RICE FOUNDATION. Because of limited resources, the foundation presently limits grants to qualified charitable programs in Lorain, Ohio, where Helen Steiner Rice was born, and Greater Cincinnati, Ohio, where Mrs. Rice lived and worked most of her life. Hopefully in the future, resources will be of sufficient size that broader geographical areas may be considered in the awarding of grants.

Because of her foresight, caring, and deep conviction of sharing, Helen Steiner Rice continues to touch a countless number of lives through foundation grants and through her inspirational poetry.

Thank you for your assistance in helping to keep Helen's dream alive and growing.

Andrea E. Cornett, Administrator

Stan Myers is an award-winning artist and member of the prestigious National Watercolor Society. His work is included in both private and corporate collections and represented by several galleries in the Midwest.

Somebody Loves You

Helen Steiner Rice

Fleming H. Revell
A Division of Baker Book House
Grand Rapids, Michigan 49516

© 1998 by The Helen Steiner Rice Foundation
All paintings are copyrighted by the artist Stan Myers and are used with
his permission

Published by Fleming H. Revell
a division of Baker Book House Company
P.O. Box 6287, Grand Rapids, MI 49516-6287

Printed in the United States of America

Library of Congress Cataloging-in-Publication Data

Rice, Helen Steiner.
    Somebody loves you / Helen Steiner Rice.
      p. cm.
    ISBN 0-8007-1747-3 (cloth)
    1. Christian poetry, American. I. Title.
PS3568.I28S58 1998
811'.54—dc21   97-12527

Contents

Somebody Loves You

Somebody loves you
   more than you know,
Somebody goes with you
   wherever you go,
Somebody really
   and truly cares
And lovingly listens
   to all of your prayers.
Don't doubt for a minute
   that this is not true,
For God loves His children
   and takes care of them too,
And all of His treasures
   are yours to share
If you love Him completely
   and show Him you care,
And if you walk in His footsteps
   and have the faith to believe,
There's nothing you ask for
   that you will not receive.

Enfolded in His Love

The love of God surrounds us
Like the air we breathe around us—
As near as a heartbeat, as close as a prayer,
And whenever we need Him, He'll always be there.

God's Love

God's love is like an island
   in life's ocean vast and wide—
A peaceful, quiet shelter
   from the restless, rising tide.

God's love is like an anchor
   when the angry billows roll—
A mooring in the storms of life,
   a stronghold for the soul.

God's love is like a fortress
   and we seek protection there
When the waves of tribulation
   seem to drown us in despair.

God's love is like a harbor
   where our souls can find sweet rest
From the struggle and the tension
   of life's fast and futile quest.

God's love is like a beacon
   burning bright with faith and prayer,
And through the changing scenes of life
   we can find a haven there.

One Thing Never Changes

The seasons swiftly come and go
    and with them comes the thought
Of all the various changes
    that time in flight has brought.
But one thing never changes,
    it remains the same forever—
God truly loves His children
    and He will forsake them never.

God Is No Stranger

God is no stranger in a faraway place,
He's as close as the wind that blows 'cross my face.
It's true I can't see the wind as it blows,
But I feel it around me and my heart surely knows
That God's mighty hand can be felt every minute
For there is nothing on earth that God isn't in it—
The sky and the stars, the waves and the sea,
The dew on the grass, the leaves on a tree
Are constant reminders of God and His nearness,
Proclaiming His presence with crystal-like clearness.
So how could I think God was far, far away
When I feel Him beside me every hour of the day,
And I've plenty of reasons to know God's my Friend
And this is one friendship that time cannot end.

Wondrous Evidence

Who can see the dawn break through
Without a glimpse of heaven and You,
For who but God could make the day
And gently put the night away.

Mystery and Miracle

———— ❧ ————

In the beauty of a snowflake,
    falling softly on the land,
Is the mystery and the miracle
    of God's great, creative hand.

If We but Believe

———— ❧ ————

If we put our problems in God's hand,
There is nothing we need understand.
It is enough to just believe
That what we need we will receive.

He Loves You

It's amazing and incredible,
  but it's as true as it can be,
God loves and understands us all
  and that means you and me.
His grace is all sufficient
  for both the young and old,
For the lonely and the timid,
  for the brash and for the bold.
His love knows no exceptions,
  so never feel excluded,
No matter who or what you are
  your name has been included.
And no matter what your past has been,
  trust God to understand,
And no matter what your problem is,
  just place it in His hand,
For in all of our unloveliness
  this great God loves us still,
He loved us since the world began
  and what's more, He always will.

God's Presence

And so today I walk with God
because I love Him so.
If I have faith and trust in Him,
there's nothing I need know.

Seek First His Kingdom

Always remember
   that whatever betide you
The power of God
   is always beside you.
If friends disappoint you
   and plans go astray
And nothing works out
   in just the right way,
If you feel you have failed
   in achieving your goal
And that life wrongly placed you
   in an unfitting role,
Take heart and stand tall
   and think who you are,
For God is your Father
   and no one can bar
Or keep you from reaching
   your desired success

Or withhold the joy
   that is yours to possess.
For with God on your side
   it matters not who
Is working to keep
   life's good things from you,
For you need nothing more
   than God's guidance and love
To insure you the things
   that you're most worthy of.
So trust in His wisdom
   and follow His ways
And be not concerned
   with the world's empty praise,
But seek first His kingdom
   and you will possess
The world's greatest riches,
   which is true happiness.

Our Refuge and Strength

The Lord is our salvation
   and our strength in every fight,
Our Redeemer and Protector,
   our eternal guiding light.
He has promised to sustain us,
   He's our refuge from all harms,
And underneath this refuge
   are His everlasting arms.

The Reflections of God

The silent stars in timeless skies,
The wonderment in children's eyes,
The autumn haze, the breath of spring,
The chirping song the crickets sing,
A rosebud in a slender vase
Are all reflections of God's face.

God's Hand Is Always There

I am perplexed
And often vexed
And sometimes I cry
And sadly sigh,
But do not think, dear Father above,
I question You or Your unchanging love—
It's just sometimes when I reach out
You seem to be nowhere about.
And while I'm sure that You love me still
And I know in my heart that You always will,
Somehow I feel that I cannot reach You
And though I get down on my knees and beseech You,
I cannot bring You closer to me
And I feel adrift on life's raging sea.
But though I cannot find Your hand
To lead me on to the Promised Land,
I still believe with all my being
Your hand is there beyond my seeing.

Faith Is the Key to Heaven

Oh, Father, grant once more to us
A simple, childlike faith and trust,
Forgetting color, race, and creed
And seeing only the heart's deep need,
For faith alone can save our souls
And lead us on to higher goals,
For there's but one unfailing course—
We win by faith and not by force.

Live by Faith

When everything is pleasant and bright
And the things we do turn out just right,
We feel without question that God is real,
For when we are happy how good we feel.
But when the tides turn and gone is the song
And misfortune comes and our plans go wrong,
Doubt creeps in and we start to wonder
And our thoughts about God are torn asunder—
For we feel deserted in time of deep stress,
Without God's presence to assure us and bless,
And it is then when our senses are reeling
We realize clearly it's faith and not feeling—
For it takes great faith to patiently wait,
Believing God comes not too soon or too late.

God's Care

When trouble comes,
   as it does to us all,
God is so great
   and we are so small,
But there is nothing
   that we need know
If we have faith
   that wherever we go
God will be waiting
   to help us bear
Our pain and sorrow,
   our suffering and care—
For no pain or suffering
   is ever too much
To yield itself
   to God's merciful touch.

The Master Builder

God is the Master Builder,
　His plans are perfect and true,
And when He sends you sorrow,
　it's part of His plan for you,
For all things work together
　to complete the master plan,
For God up in His heaven
　can see what's best for man.

Love Divine, All Loves Excelling

In a myriad of miraculous ways
God shapes our lives and changes our days,
Beyond our will or even knowing
God keeps our spirit ever growing,
For lights and shadows, sun and rain,
Sadness and gladness, joy and pain,
Combine to make our lives complete
And give us victory through defeat.
Oh, "Love Divine, All Loves Excelling,"
In troubled hearts You just keep dwelling,
Patiently waiting for a prodigal son
To say at last, "Thy will be done."

Life Is a Highway

Life is a highway
    on which the years go by.
Sometimes the road is level,
    sometimes the hills are high.
But as we travel onward
    to a future that's unknown,
We can make each mile we travel
    a heavenly stepping-stone.

Today, Tomorrow, and Always

In sickness or health,
    in suffering and pain,
In storm-laden skies,
    in sunshine and rain,
God always is there
    to lighten your way
And lead you through darkness
    to a much brighter day.

A Time of Renewal

No one likes to be sick
   and yet we know
It takes sunshine and rain
   to make flowers grow.
And if we never were sick
   and never felt pain,
We'd be like a desert
   without any rain,
And who wants a life
   that is barren and dry
With never a cloud
   to darken the sky,
For continuous sun
   goes unrecognized
Like the blessings God sends
   that are often disguised,
For sometimes a sickness
   that seems so distressing
Is a time of renewal
   and a spiritual blessing.

Daily Prayers Dissolve Your Cares

I meet God in the morning
    and go with Him through the day,
Then in the stillness of the night
    before sleep comes I pray
That God will just take over
    all the problems I couldn't solve,
And in the peacefulness of sleep
    my cares will all dissolve,
So when I open up my eyes
    to greet another day,
I'll find myself renewed in strength
    and there will open up a way
To meet what seemed impossible
    for me to solve alone,
And once again I'll be assured
    I am never on my own.
For if we try to stand alone,
    we are weak and we will fall,

For God is always greatest
    when we're helpless, lost, and small,
But no day is unmeetable
    if, on rising, our first thought
Is to thank God for the blessings
    that His loving care has brought—
For there can be no failures
    or hopeless, unsaved sinners
If we enlist the help of God,
    who makes all losers winners.
So meet Him in the morning
    and go with Him through the day,
And thank Him for His guidance
    each evening when you pray,
And if you follow faithfully
    this daily way to pray,
You will never in your lifetime
    face another hopeless day.

For the Ill or Soul Sick

Sometimes when we
   are physically ill
We're prone to resort
   to a tonic or pill,
Neglecting to place
   ourselves in God's care
By seeking His help
   on the wings of prayer—
For God can remove
   our uncertain fear
And replace our worry
   with healing cheer.
So close your eyes
   and open your heart
And let God come in
   and freely impart
A brighter outlook
   and new courage too,
As His spiritual sunshine
   smiles on you.

How Little We Know

God, how little I was really aware
Of the pain and the trouble and deep despair
That floods the hearts of those in pain
As they struggle to cope but feel it's in vain,
Crushed with frustration and with no haven to seek,
With broken spirits and bodies so weak,
And yet they forget Christ suffered and died
And hung on the cross and was crucified,
And He did it all so some happy day,
When the sorrows of earth have all passed away,
We who have suffered will forever be free
To live with God in eternity.

Secure in Him

Faith makes it wholly possible
to quietly endure
The violent world around us
for in God we are secure.

A Firm Foundation of Faith

———— ⁂ ————

Faith is a force that is greater
than knowledge or power or skill,
And the darkest defeat turns to triumph
if we trust in God's wisdom and will.

The House of Prayer

———— ⁂ ————

The house of prayer is no farther away
Than the quiet spot where you kneel and pray,
For the heart is a temple when God is there
As you place yourself in His loving care.

We Never Walk Alone

What more can we ask of the Savior
    than to know we are never alone—
That His mercy and love are unfailing
    and He makes all our problems His own.

In God Is My Strength

My earthly load I could not bear
If You were not there to share
All the pain, despair, and sorrow
That almost makes me dread tomorrow,
For I am often weak and weary
And life is dark and bleak and dreary.
But somehow when I realize
That He who made the sea and skies
And holds the whole world in His hand
Has my small soul in His command,
It gives me strength to try once more
To press on toward the heavenly door
Where I will live forevermore
With friends and loved ones I adore.

God's Assurance Gives Us Endurance

My blessings are so many,
   my troubles are so few,
How can I feel discouraged
   when I know that I have You,
And I have the sweet assurance
   that I'll never stand alone
If I but keep remembering
   I am Yours and Yours alone?
So in this world of trouble
   with darkness all around,
Take my hand and lead me
   until I stand on higher ground,
And help me to endure the storms
   that keep raging deep inside me
And make me more aware each day
   that no evil can betide me
If I remain undaunted,
   though the billows sweep and roll,
Knowing I have Your assurance
   there's a haven for my soul,
For anything and everything
   can somehow be endured
If Your presence is beside me
   and lovingly assured.

People's Problems

Everyone has problems
  in this restless world of care,
Everyone grows weary
  with the crosses they must bear.
Everyone is troubled
  and their skies are overcast
As they try to face the future
  while still dwelling in the past.
But the people with their problems
  only listen with one ear,
For people only listen
  to the things they want to hear,
And they only hear the kind of things
  they are able to believe,
And the answers that are God's to give
  they're not ready to receive.
So while the people's problems
  keep growing every day
And humans try to solve them
  in their own willful way,

God seeks to help and watches,
    waiting always patiently
To help them solve their problems,
    whatever they may be,
So people of all nations
    may at last become aware
That God will solve their problems
    through faith and hope and prayer.

Under God's Control

Many trials and troubles
　　are scattered on our way,
Daily little crosses
　　are a part of every day.
But the troubles we have suffered
　　are over, past, and through,
So why should bygone happenings
　　keep gravely troubling you?
And the problems that beset us
　　in the now and present hour,
We need not try to solve alone
　　without God's grace and power,
And those scheduled for tomorrow
　　still belong to God alone—
They are still unborn and formless
　　and a part of the unknown.
So let us face the trouble
　　that is ours this present minute
And count on God to help us
　　and put His mercy in it
And forget the past and future
　　and dwell wholly on today,
For God controls the future
　　and He will direct our way.

Put Your Problem in God's Hands

Although it sometimes seems to us
    our prayers have not been heard,
God always knows our every need
    without a single word,
And He will not forsake us
    even though the way seems steep,
For always He is near to us,
    a tender watch to keep,
And in good time He'll answer us
    and in His love He'll send
Greater things than we have asked
    and blessings without end.
So though we do not understand
    why trouble comes to man,
Can we not be contented
    just to know that it's God's plan?

He Answers All Our Prayers

There's no problem too big
    and no question too small,
Just ask God in faith
    and He'll answer them all—
Not always at once,
    so be patient and wait,
For God never comes
    too soon or too late.
So trust in His wisdom
    and believe in His Word,
For no prayer's unanswered
    and no prayer unheard.

Be Not Dismayed

It's a dismal, dreary morning
   and as I sometimes do,
I feel a little dreary
   and kinda downcast too,
For let nobody tell you
   that life's a happy song
And that we just keep smiling
   when everything goes wrong,
For it would not be natural
   to always wear a smile,
For a smile would be a silly grin
   if it covered up a trial,
For there are certain periods
   when the soul is sweetly sad
As it contemplates the mystery
   of both good times and bad.

We're not really discontented
   and we are never unaware
That the good Lord up in heaven
   has us always in His care,
But the soul of man is restless
   and it just keeps longing for
A haven that is safe and sure
   that will last forevermore.
And as I sit here writing this
   a thought passed through my mind—
Why dwell on past or future
   or what's ahead or gone behind?
Just follow God unquestioningly
   because you love Him so,
For if you trust His judgment
   there is nothing you need know.

My Daily Prayer

God, be my resting place and my protection
In hours of trouble, defeat, and dejection.
May I never give way to self-pity and sorrow,
May I always be sure of a better tomorrow,
May I stand undaunted come what may
Secure in the knowledge I have only to pray
And ask my Creator and Father above
To keep me serene in His grace and His love.

This Is Just a Resting Place

Sometimes the road of life seems long
   as we travel through the years,
And with a heart that's broken
   and eyes brimful of tears,
We falter in our weariness
   and sink beside the way,
But God leans down and whispers,
   "Child, there'll be another day."
And the road will grow much smoother
   and much easier to face,
So do not be disheartened—
   this is just a resting place.

Trust and Believe

Whatever our problems, troubles, and sorrows,
If we trust in the Lord, there'll be brighter tomorrows,
For there's nothing too much for the great God to do,
And all that He asks or expects from you
Is faith that's unshaken by tribulations and tears
That keeps growing stronger along with the years,
Content in the knowledge that God knows best
And that trouble and sorrow are only a test—
For without God's testing of our soul
It never would reach its ultimate goal.
So keep on believing, whatever betide you,
Knowing that God will be with you to guide you,
And all that He promised will be yours to receive
If you trust Him completely and always believe.

Recognize His Blessings

Stop wishing for things
  you complain you have not
And start making the best
  of all that you've got.

With God All Things Are Possible

Nothing is ever too hard to do
If your faith is strong and your purpose is true.
So never give up and never stop,
Just journey on to the mountaintop.

My Garden of Prayer

My garden beautifies my yard
   and adds fragrance to the air,
But it is also my cathedral
   and my quiet place of prayer.
So little do we realize
   that the glory and the power
Of He who made the universe
   lies hidden in a flower.

Help Us to See and Understand

God, give us wider vision
  to see and understand
That both the sun and showers
  are gifts from Thy great hand,
And when our lives are overcast
  with trouble and with care,
Give us faith to see beyond
  the dark clouds of despair,

And give us strength to rise above
   the mist of doubt and fear,
To recognize the hidden smile
   behind each burning tear.
Teach us that it takes the showers
   to make the flowers grow,
And only in the storms of life
   when the winds of trouble blow
Can we too reach maturity
   and grow in faith and grace
And gain the strength and courage
   to enable us to face
Sunny days as well as rain,
   high peaks as well as low,
Knowing that the April showers
   will make the May flowers grow—
And then at last may we accept
   the sunshine and the showers,
Confident it takes them both
   to make salvation ours.

Learn to Recognize a Blessing

While it's very difficult
    for us to understand
God's intentions and His purpose
    and the workings of His hand,
If we observe the miracles
    that happen every day,
We cannot help but be convinced
    that in His wondrous way
God makes what seemed unbearable
    and painful and distressing
Easily acceptable
    when we view it as a blessing.

Sorrow Helps Our Souls to Grow

There's a lot of comfort in the thought
  that sorrow, grief, and woe
Are sent into our lives sometimes
  to help our souls to grow,
For through the depths of sorrow
  comes understanding love,
And peace and truth and comfort
  are sent from God above.

No Crown without a Cross

We all have those days
   that are dismal and dreary
And we feel sorta blue
   and lonely and weary,
But we have to admit
   that life is worth living
And God gives us reasons
   for daily thanksgiving,
For life's an experience
   God's children go through
That's made up of gladness
   and much sadness too.
But we have to know both
   the bitter and sweet

If we want a good life
   that is full and complete,
For each trial we suffer
   and every shed tear
Just gives us new strength
   to persevere
As we climb the steep hills
   along life's way
That lead us at last
   to that wonderful day
Where the cross we have carried
   becomes a crown
And at last we can lay
   our burden down.

Trust in His Wisdom

Since God forgives us,
    we too must forgive
And resolve to do better
    each day that we live
By constantly trying
    to be like Him more nearly
And to trust in His wisdom
    and love Him more dearly.

God's Peace and Calm

With the Lord as your shepherd
 you have all that you need,
For if you follow in His footsteps
 wherever He may lead,
He will guard and guide and keep you
 in His loving, watchful care,
And when traveling in dark valleys,
 Your shepherd will be there.
His goodness is unfailing,
 His kindness knows no end,
For the Lord is a Good Shepherd
 on whom you can depend.
So when your heart is troubled,
 you'll find quiet peace and calm
If you open up the Bible
 and read the Twenty-third Psalm.

Be of Good Cheer

Since fear and dread and worry
    cannot help in any way,
It's much healthier and happier
    to be cheerful every day,
And if we'll only try it
    we will find, without a doubt,
A cheerful attitude's something
    no one should be without—
For when the heart is cheerful
    it cannot be filled with fear,
And without fear the way ahead
    seems more distinct and clear,
And we realize there's nothing
    we need ever face alone,
For our heavenly Father loves us
    and our problems are His own.

Thy Will Be Done

God did not promise sun without rain,
    light without darkness, or joy without pain—
He only promised us strength for the day
    when the darkness comes and we lose our way,
For only through sorrow do we grow more aware
    that God is our refuge in times of despair.
For when we are happy and life's bright and fair,
    we often forget to kneel down in prayer,
But God seems much closer and needed much more
    when trouble and sorrow stand outside our door—
For then we seek shelter in His wondrous love
    and we ask Him to send us help from above.
And that is the reason we know it is true
    that bright, shining hours and dark, sad ones too,
Are part of the plan God made for each one,
    and all we can pray is "Thy will be done."

God's Mighty Handiwork

"The earth is the Lord's
and the fullness thereof"—
It speaks of His greatness,
it sings of His love,
It whispers of mysteries
we cannot comprehend
Of a beautiful land
where life has no end.

Anxious Prayers

When we are deeply disturbed
  and our mind is filled with doubt,
And we struggle to find a solution
  but there seems to be no way out,
We futilely keep on trying
  to untangle our web of distress,
But our own little, puny efforts
  meet with very little success.
And finally exhausted and weary,
  discouraged and downcast and low,
With no foreseeable answer
  and with no other place to go,
We kneel down in sheer desperation
  and slowly and stumblingly pray
Then impatiently wait for an answer,
  which we fully expect right away.

And then when God does not answer,
  in one, sudden instant we say,
"God does not seem to be listening,
  so why should we bother to pray?"
But God can't get through to the anxious
  who are much too impatient to wait,
You have to believe in God's promise
  that He comes not too soon or too late,
For whether God answers promptly
  or delays in answering your prayer,
You must have faith to believe Him
  and to know in your heart He'll be there.
So be not impatient or hasty,
  just trust in the Lord and believe,
For whatever you ask in faith and love
  in abundance you are sure to receive.

Learn to Rest

We all need short vacations
    in life's fast and maddening race—
An interlude of quietness
    from the constant, jet-age pace.
So when your day is pressure packed
    and your hours are all too few,
Just close your eyes and meditate
    and let God talk to you,
For when we keep on pushing,
    we're not following in God's way—
We are foolish, selfish robots
    mechanized to fill each day
With unimportant trivia
    that makes life more complex
And gives us greater problems
    to irritate and vex.

So when your nervous network
  becomes a tangled mess,
Just close your eyes in silent prayer
  and ask the Lord to bless
Each thought that you are thinking,
  each decision you must make,
As well as every word you speak
  and every step you take,
For only by the grace of God
  can you gain self-control,
And only meditative thoughts
  can restore your peace of soul.

In God's Care

The better you know God, the better you feel,
For to learn more about Him and discover He's real
Can wholly, completely, and miraculously change,
Reshape and remake and then rearrange
Your mixed-up, miserable, and unhappy life
Adrift on the sea of sin-sickened strife.
But when you once know this Man of goodwill,
He will calm your life and say, "Peace, be still."
So open your heart's door and let Christ come in
And He'll give you new life and free you from sin—
And there is no joy that can ever compare
With the joy of knowing you're in God's care.

How to Find Happiness

Happiness is something that is never far away,
It's as close as the things we do and we say.
So start out today with a smile on your face
And make this old world a happier place.

The Gift of Love

There are things we cannot measure,
    like the depths of waves and sea
And the heights of stars in heaven
    and the joy You bring to me.
Like eternity's long endlessness
    and the sunset's golden hue,
There is no way to measure
    the love I have for You.

The Meaning of True Love

It is sharing and caring,
Giving and forgiving,
Loving and being loved,
Walking hand in hand,
Talking heart to heart,
Seeing through each other's eyes,
Laughing together,
Weeping together,
Praying together,
And always trusting
And believing
And thanking God
For each other . . .
For love that is shared
    is a beautiful thing—
It enriches the soul
    and makes the heart sing.

The Gift of Lasting Love

Love is much more than a tender caress
And more than bright hours of gay happiness,
For a lasting love is made up of sharing
Both hours that are joyous and also despairing.
It's made up of patience and deep understanding
And never of selfish and stubborn demanding.
It's made up of climbing the steep hills together
And facing with courage life's stormiest weather.
And nothing on earth or in heaven can part
A love that has grown to be part of the heart,
And just like the sun and the stars and the sea,
This love will go on through eternity—
For true love lives on when earthly things die,
For it's part of the spirit that soars to the sky.

The Joy of Unselfish Giving

Time is not measured
   by the years that you live
But by the deeds that you do
   and the joy that you give.
And each day as it comes
   brings a chance to each one
To love to the fullest,
   leaving nothing undone
That would brighten the life
   or lighten the load
Of some weary traveler
   lost on life's road.
So what does it matter
   how long we may live
If as long as we live
   we unselfishly give.

Not by the Years We Live

From one day to another
   God will gladly give
To everyone who seeks Him
   and tries each day to live
A little bit more closely
   to God and to each other,
Seeing everyone who passes
   as a neighbor, friend, or brother,
Not only joy and happiness
   but the faith to meet each trial
Not with fear and trepidation
   but with an inner smile,
For we know life's never measured
   by how many years we live
But by the kindly things we do
   and the happiness we give.

Always a Tomorrow

How often we wish for another chance
  to make a fresh beginning,
A chance to blot out our mistakes
  and change failure into winning—
And it does not take a special time
  to make a brand-new start,
It only takes the deep desire
  to try with all our heart
To live a little better
  and to always be forgiving
And to add a little sunshine
  to the world in which we're living.
So never give up in despair
  and think that you are through,
For there's always a tomorrow
  and a chance to start anew.

Take Time to Be Kind

Kindness is a virtue
   given by the Lord,
It pays dividends in happiness
   and joy is its reward.
For if you practice kindness
   in all you say and do,
The Lord will wrap His kindness
   around your heart and you,
And wrapped within His kindness
   you are sheltered and secure,
And under His direction
   your way is safe and sure.

Love One Another

"Love one another as I have loved you"
May seem impossible to do—
But if you will try to trust and believe
Great are the joys that you will receive,
For love makes us patient, understanding, and kind,
And we judge with our hearts and not with our mind,
For as soon as love enters the heart's open door,
The faults we once saw are not there anymore,
And the things that seemed wrong begin to look right
When viewed in the softness of love's gentle light.
For love works in ways that are wondrous and strange,
And there is nothing in life that love cannot change,
And all that God promised will someday come true
When you love one another the way He loves you.

What Is Love?

———— ✳ ————

What is love?
   No words can define it,
It's something so great
   only God could design it.
Wonder of wonders,
   beyond our conception,
And only in God
   can love find true perfection,
For love is enduring
   and patient and kind,
It judges all things
   with the heart, not the mind.
And love can transform
   the most commonplace

Into beauty and splendor
   and sweetness and grace,
For love is unselfish,
   giving more than it takes,
And no matter what happens
   love never forsakes.
It's faithful and trusting
   and always believing,
Guileless and honest
   and never deceiving.
Yes, love is beyond
   what we can define,
For love is immortal
   and God's gift is divine.

A Prayer for Those We Love

"Our Father Who art in heaven,"
    hear this little prayer
And reach across the miles today
    that stretch from here to there,
So I may feel much closer
    to those I'm fondest of
And they may know I think of them
    with thankfulness and love.
And help all people everywhere
    who must often dwell apart
To know that they're together
    in the haven of the heart.